John Thompson's
SUPPLEMENTARY PIANO COURSE
with
MELODY ALL THE WAY
A PREPARATORY BOOK BASED ON FAMILIAR AIRS

Contents

To the Teacher

1. First teach the KEYS in Groups of Three—in alphabetical order since most beginners already know their letters in that form.

First Group

Second Group

Third Group

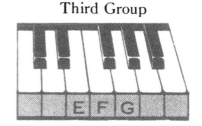

As each group is learned have the pupil locate ALL THE KEYS OF THAT PARTICULAR GROUP in each and every octave on the Keyboard. The importance of this is obvious. Thus *all* the White Keys can be taught in one session.

2. Next teach the lesson on ELEMENTS OF NOTATION, page 3.

3. Present the NOTES page 4.

To make certain that the pupil is actually playing by note, it should be required that each example be performed in two ways—first by having the pupil count aloud, then by singing the letter-names of the notes while playing. Later it can also be done as a Song, making use of the words.

4. It is an excellent idea to have the student play each example in various octaves—up and down—from the one in which it is written thus becoming familiar with the entire range of the Keyboard.

5. This Preparatory Book may be used interchangeably with, or supplementary to, "TEACHING LITTLE FINGERS TO PLAY"—the Preparatory Book in the same author's Modern Course for the Piano.

6. Do not overlook the value of using a Writing Book for home-work. It not only develops more certainty in the matter of Notation but also promotes the ability to read at sight. John Thompson's NOTE SPELLER is designed especially for beginners. It progresses in *exactly the same order* as the lessons at the keyboard and provides practice in writing Clef Signs, Bar Lines, Measures, Time Values, Signatures, Notation, Rests, Accidentals, Sight Reading, Transposition, Dictation and Melody Writing.

Copyright, MCMXLIX, by The Willis Music Co.
International Copyright Secured
Printed in U. S. A.

J. T.

Elements of Notation

THE GRAND STAFF
(on which the music is written)

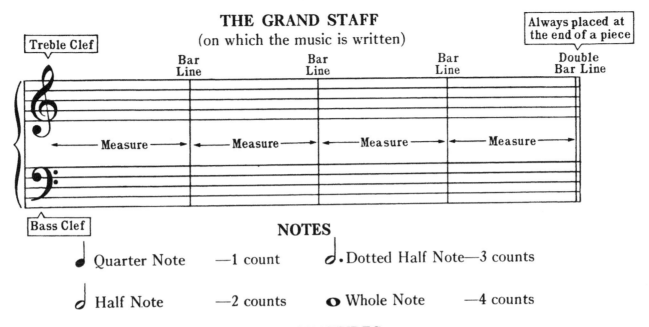

Treble Clef

Bar Line

Bar Line

Bar Line

Always placed at the end of a piece

Double Bar Line

Measure — Measure — Measure — Measure

Bass Clef

NOTES

Quarter Note —1 count   Dotted Half Note—3 counts

Half Note —2 counts   Whole Note —4 counts

TIME SIGNATURES

The TIME SIGNATURE is placed at the beginning of each piece.
The upper figure tells how many counts to each measure.
The lower figure shows the *kind* of note which gets one count.

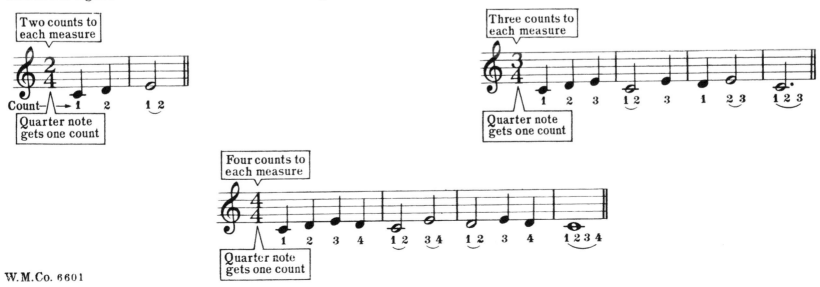

Two counts to each measure

Count— 1 2 1 2

Quarter note gets one count

Three counts to each measure

1 2 3 1 2 3 1 2 3 1 2 3

Quarter note gets one count

Four counts to each measure

1 2 3 4 1 2 3 4 1 2 3 4 1 2 3 4

Quarter note gets one count

W.M.Co. 6601

The Musical Bank

THE MUSICAL BANK OF AMERICA

| Quarter Notes
1 count each | Half Notes
2 counts each | Dotted Half Notes
3 counts each | Whole Notes
4 counts each |

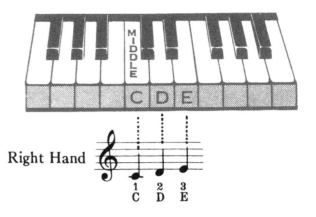

Right Hand

1 2 3
C D E

How to Practice

First—Count the Time aloud as you play.

Next—Recite the letter-names of the Notes while playing.

Two Counts to a Measure

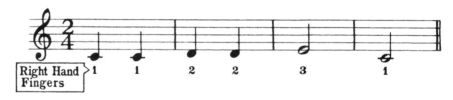

Right Hand Fingers   1   1   2   2   3   1

Three Counts to a Measure

1   2   3   2   1   3   2   1

Four Counts to a Measure

3   2   1   2   3   3   2   2   3   2   1

Left Hand

3 2 1
A B C

The Three Clocks

Three different Time Signatures

Review Melodies already learned and transpose them to various octaves on the Keyboard.

As each piece is learned color the pictures with crayons.

THE DESK CLOCK

Left Hand Fingers   1   1   2   2   3   2   1   1

2 P. M.
Denver
Mountain Time

THE WALL CLOCK

3   2   1   3   2   1   3

3 P. M.
Chicago
Central Time

THE GRANDFATHER'S CLOCK

1   2   3   2   1   2   1

4 P. M.
New York
Eastern Time

W.M.Co. 6601

The Streamliner

See the train with | win-dows gleaming | whizz-ing past the | sta - tion;

By to - mor - row | she'll have jour-neyed | half a - cross the | na - tion.

This piece introduces the dotted Half Note in 4/4 Time.

Song of the Volga Boatmen

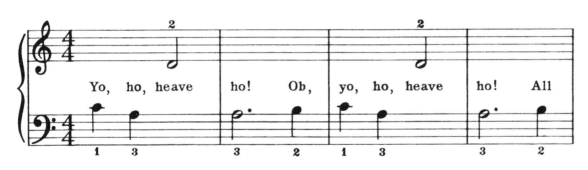

Yo, ho, heave   ho! Oh,   yo, ho, heave   ho! All

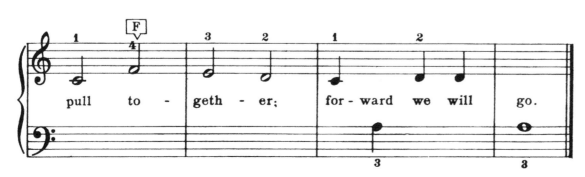

pull   to - geth - er;   for - ward   we   will   go.

Information Please

Yankee Doodle

To the Teacher: Explain *accent* and its application to the first count of each measure.

The Submarine

Always spend some time of each day reviewing the Melodies already learned.

Div-ing div-ing see the big ship clear the salt-y o-cean

Like a whale we'll see it ris-ing when it takes a no-tion.

W.M.Co. 6601

The Tie

When two notes are joined together by a Tie (curved line) the second note is not struck and the key is held for the value of both notes.

He's A Jolly Good Fellow

Rests

Rests are signs of silence.

Quarter Rest—Silent for 1 count.

Half Rest—Silent for 2 counts.

Whole Rest—Silent for 4 counts.

The Whole Rest is also used to indicate a full measure's silence, regardless of the number of counts to the measure.

The 'Cello Player

Old MacDonald Had a Farm

American Folk Song

Right Hand Position

New
Notes
E   F

New
Left Hand Position

Half Rest

Old Mac Don - ald had a farm, E - I - E - I oh!

On his farm he had some chicks E - I - E - I oh!

Teacher's Note: At this point the pupil should be assigned John Thompson's "TINY TECHNICS." It provides a course of Finger Drills *based on familiar airs.*

Introducing Eighth Notes

8th Notes

An Eighth Note gets **½** a count. Play therefore *two 8th Notes* to one count.

 Eighth Note (½ count)

 Two 8th Notes (one count)

Pieces do not always begin on the first count.

This piece begins on the fourth count.

Oh Susannah

Stephen Foster

I came to Al-a-ba-ma wid my ban-jo on my knee, I'm g'wan to Lou-si-an-a, For my own true love to see.

Teacher's Note: Explain how the last measure always balances the meter when pieces begin on other than the first count.

W. M. Co. 6601

The Flat Sign—♭

When a flat sign (♭) is placed before a
note it means the note must be *lowered*
one half-step.

This piece has an A♭ in next to the last
measure. Play the Black Key *to the
left* of A. (See Chart)

The Arkansas Traveler

Old American Tune

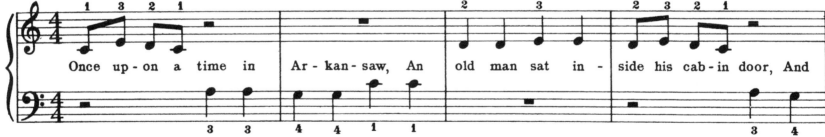

Once up-on a time in Ar-kan-saw, An old man sat in-side his cab-in door, And

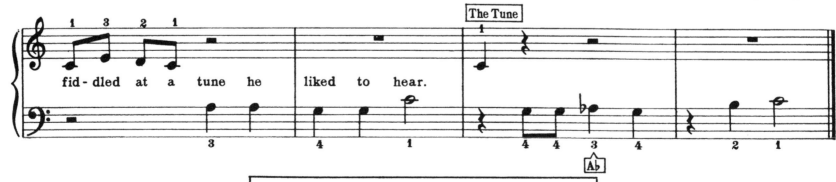

fid-dled at a tune he liked to hear.

The Tune

A♭

To the Teacher: Stress the importance of accenting the
first beat of each measure in all pieces.

W.M.Co. 6601

The Sharp Sign—♯

The sharp sign (♯) *raises* the note one half-step.

When F♯ appears in this piece, play the Black Key *to the right* of F. (See Chart)

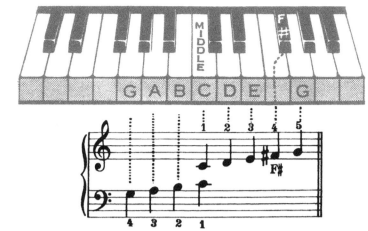

The Birthday Child

Sing, sing, what shall I sing, When I a-
wake on my birth-day? Like a blue-bird I'll
sing, A hap-py birth-day song.

W.M.Co. 6601

Key Signature

When the flat or sharp sign appears next to the Clef sign at the beginning of a piece, it becomes the *key Signature*.

In this piece all B's are flatted.

A signature of one flat is F Major.

Notice the piece ends on F in the Bass.

Old Black Joe

Stephen Foster

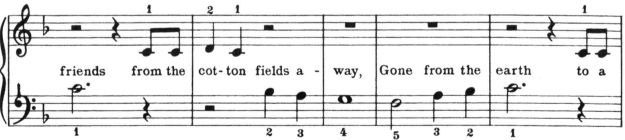

STEPHEN FOSTER

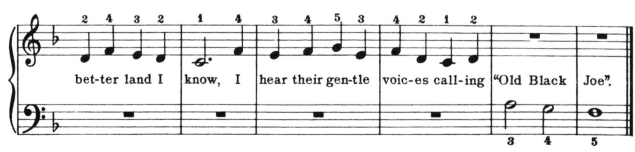

The Natural Sign—♮

The Natural (♮) cancels the effect of the sharp or flat sign.

Always play a white key when the Natural sign appears before a note.

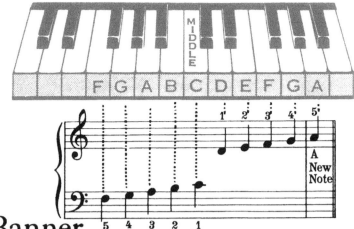

The Star Spangled Banner

Francis Scott Key

Oh say can you see, by the dawn's ear - ly light, What so proud-ly we hailed at the twi-light's last gleaming? Whose broad stripes and bright stars, thro' the per - il - ous fight, O'er the ram-parts we watched, were so gal-lant-ly stream-ing?

W.M.Co. 6601

Key Signature—One Sharp

When one sharp appears in the Key Signature, the piece is in G Major.

Notice this piece ends on G.

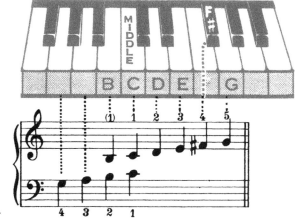

Lullaby

Brahms

gradually slower and softer

To the Teacher: Explain how and represent the same key.

Little Buttercup

From the Operetta, "Pinafore"

Gilbert-Sullivan

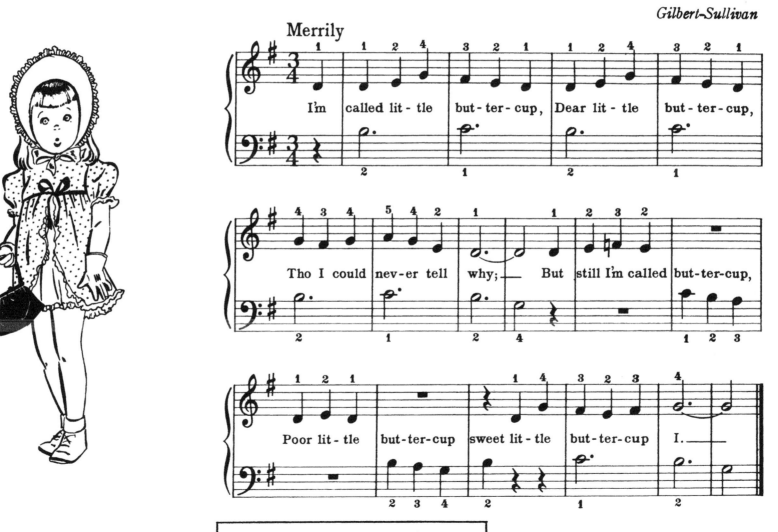

Do not forget the importance of accents.

W.M.Co. 6601

Polly Wolly Doodle

To the Teacher: Explain how ⌘ and 𝄞 represent the same key.

The Lady and the Tiger

There was a young la-dy of Ni - ger,____ Who

smiled as she rode on a ti - ger;____ They came from the ride with the

Change Position

la - dy in - side, And the smile on the face of the Ti - ger.____

Song of the Marines

In brisk March Tempo

From the halls of Mon - te - zu - ma To the shores of Trip-o - li _____ We will

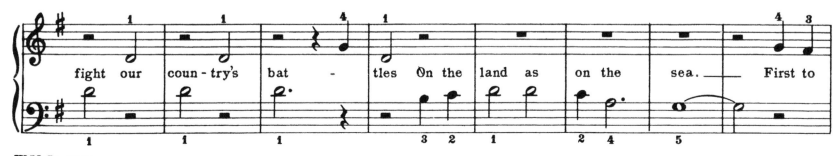

fight our coun - try's bat - tles On the land as on the sea. _____ First to

fight for right and free - dom And to keep our hon - or clean___ We are

Change Position

proud to bear the ti - tle of U - ni - ted States Ma - rines.___

The Old Gray Mare

New Bass Note

Heavy accents
in the Left Hand

Staccato and Legato

A dot over a note means *staccato* — short.

A curved line over a note means *legato*—connected.

Use the legato and staccato touches recommended by your teacher.

Reuben And Rachel

Right Hand over

Left Hand

Reuben, I have oft been thinking What a world it then would be, If all men could be transported Leagues beyond the Northern sea.

Be very careful of the fingering.
Key of D— Two Sharps—F♯ and C♯

W.M.Co. 6601

Both Hands Playing in Treble Clef

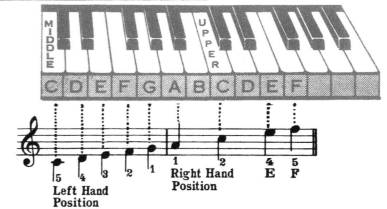

The Pause Sign

This sign placed over a note means that the player should pause for a moment, then proceed as before.

The Minstrel Boy

Thomas Moore

W.M.Co. 6601

Christmas Duet

(Teacher's or Parent's Part)

It Came Upon the Midnight Clear

Richard S. Willis

Slowly – *with much expression*

Christmas Duet

(Pupil's Part)

It Came Upon the Midnight Clear

Slowly— *with much expression*

Richard S. Willis

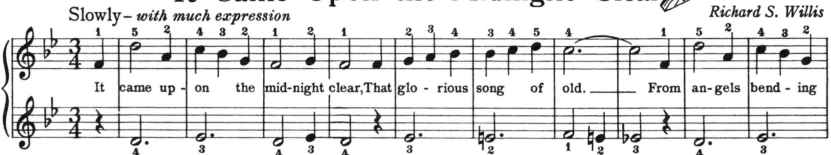

It came up-on the mid-night clear, That glo-rious song of old.____ From an-gels bend-ing

near the earth, To touch their harps of gold;____ "Peace on the earth, good will to men, From

Heav'-n's all gra-cious King"; The world in sol-emn still-ness lay To hear the an-gels sing.____

Key of Bb—Two flats—Bb and Eb

Jingle Bells

Good Night Ladies

Bill Grogan's Goat

College Song

Short'nin' Bread

In quick tempo

Southern Song

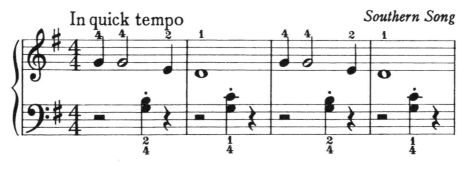

From

In the Hall of the Mountain King

Ed. Grieg

From

Marche Slave

Tschaikowsky

Chop Sticks

(With Variations)

Variation

Turkey in the Straw

In lively tempo

Old American Jig

To be sure of the Time, play these four measures first *without* the Ties, thus   later

The Villain

Traditional

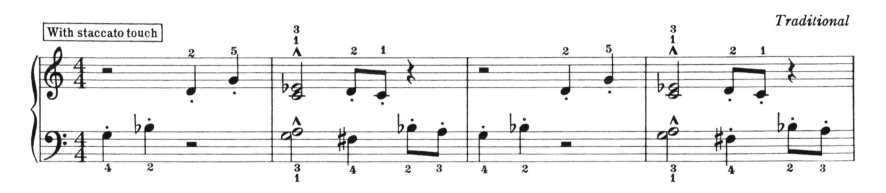

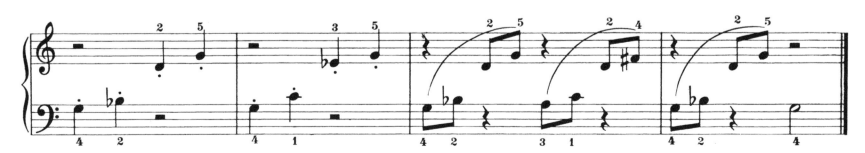

W.M.Co. 6601

Dixie

Dan D. Emmett

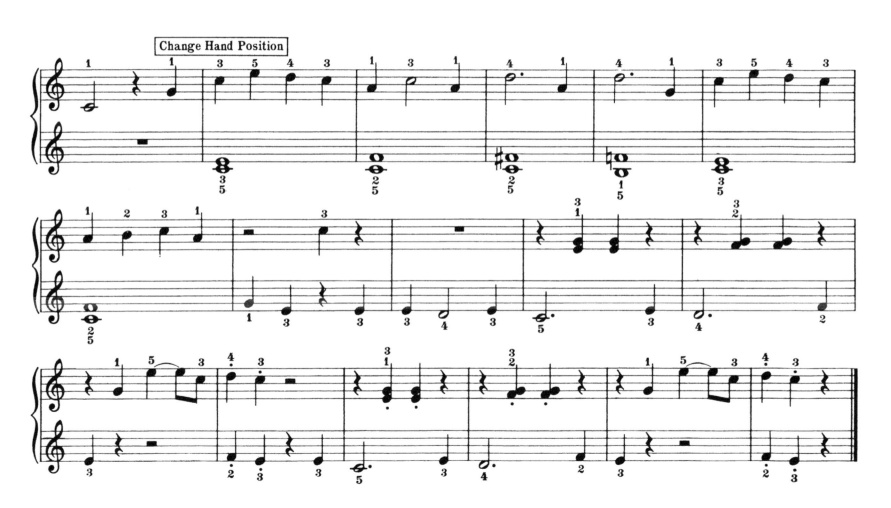

Certificate of Merit

This certifies that

....

has successfully completed

THE PREPARATORY BOOK

OF

"MELODY ALL THE WAY"

and is eligible for promotion to

BOOK 1-a

....
Teacher

Date........................